UNREAL BUT REAL ANIMALS

INCREDIBLY COLOURFUL CREATURES

by Megan Cooley Peterson

raintree
a Capstone company — publishers for children

Raintree is an imprint of Capstone Global Library Limited, a company incorporated in England and Wales having its registered office at 264 Banbury Road, Oxford, OX2 7DY – Registered company number: 6695582

www.raintree.co.uk
myorders@raintree.co.uk

ISBN 978 1 3982 4487 0 (hardback)
ISBN 978 1 3982 4488 7 (paperback)

Editorial Credits
Editor: Erika L. Shores; Designer: Hilary Wacholz; Media Researchers: Jo Miller and Pam Mitsakos; Production Specialist: Tori Abraham

Image Credits
Alamy: Eng Wah Teo, 23, George Grill, 25, Jason Edwards, 13, Paul Harrison, 4; Science Source: Adam Fletcher, 29, Gary Meszaros, 19; Shutterstock: A. Kehinde, 17, ArCaLu, 5, 14, Cingular, Cover (top), Elocin Nadroj, Cover (bottom), fenkieandreas, 11, fntproject, 27, Jay Ondreicka, 18, 26, Jesus Cobaleda, 7, Joe Belanger, 9, Kletr, 10, nwdph, 15, Sara Nadeea, 6, slowmotiongli, 21
Design Elements
Shutterstock: Cassel

All internet sites appearing in back matter were available and accurate when this book was sent to press.

British Library Cataloguing in Publication Data
A full catalogue record for this book is available from the British Library.

Printed and bound in India

CONTENTS

Words in **bold** are in the glossary.

WARNING: BRIGHT COLOURS AHEAD

Move over, brown bears. Step aside, grey elephants. The flashy creatures in this book aren't afraid of a little colour – or a lot! Some are so colourful they almost look fake. But all of the animals in this book are real.

COLOURS IN THE SEA

ONE-TWO PUNCH

One of nature's best hunters punches like a little boxer. The peacock mantis shrimp attacks with its hammer claws.

These punches move as fast as a bullet.

FACT

The peacock mantis shrimp has unusual eyes. They can look in two directions at the same time. Each eye moves on its own.

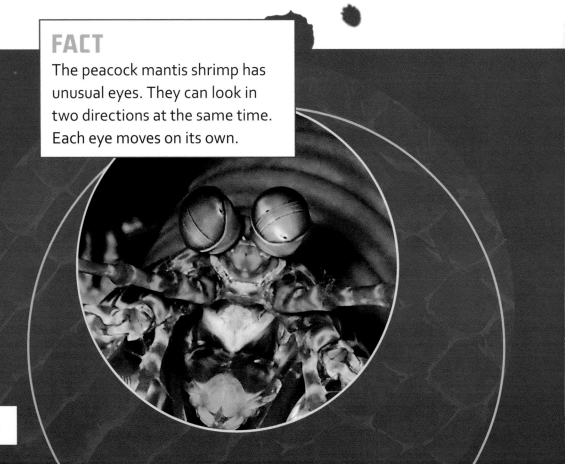

The mantis shrimp's colourful body blends in with the **coral reef**. It sneaks up on its food. Wham! It bashes through the animal's shell.

SUNGLASSES NEEDED

Grab some sunglasses when you look at this animal. It seems to glow. Spanish shawl sea slugs have **neon** purple bodies. On top grows an orange, finger-like fringe.

The food these sea slugs eat gives them their amazing colours. Spanish shawls also get stinging **cells** from their food. They store them in their fringe. Zap! An animal got too close!

FACT
Spanish shawl sea slugs also use their fringe to breathe.

fringe

COLOUR MAZE

How do you know that mandarinfish like mazes? Because they wear them on their bodies. Red, orange and yellow lines swirl across these fish. The bright colours let other animals know they should stay away because the fish taste bad.

COLOURS IN THE TREES

HANDS OFF!

Don't eat me! The wattle cup caterpillar's dazzling colours send a warning. Its colours scare off most attackers. Sharp **spines** also get the job done. Each spine is filled with **venom**. Getting stung by this insect hurts!

FACT
The wattle cup caterpillar turns into a cream and brown moth. Boring. But its dull colours keep it hidden.

STEALING THE SHOW

Here's a bird that takes colourful to the next level. Its rainbow-like feathers come in eight colours. Both the male and female lilac-breasted roller are brightly coloured.

Rollers are super fliers. They sit high in the tops of trees. Lizards and insects crawl on the ground below. The birds then dive for the kill.

SMELLY WORK OF ART

Can an insect be a work of art? Check out the Picasso bug. It has spots of blue, green and red. These colours tell other animals to back off. The bug can also let out a horrible smell when it's scared. Hungry animals move on to a less stinky meal.

FACT

The Picasso bug was named after Pablo Picasso. This famous artist painted with bright colours.

NOW YOU SEE ME, NOW YOU DON'T

Is that flying candy floss? No, it's the rosy maple moth. It is bright pink and yellow. This clever insect can hide in plain sight. Rosy maple moths live in maple trees. Their bodies look like maple tree seed cases. Birds can't see them.

SHOWING OFF

These birds look like they've been painted! Gouldian finches have red, yellow or black heads. Males have brighter purple feathers than females. Males puff up and bob their heads. They use their beautiful feathers to attract a mate.

FACT
Gouldian finches get their bright colours from the seeds they eat.

COLOURS ON THE GROUND

SCALY SECRETS

This snake's bright blue and red scales hide its secret weapon. The Asian blue coral snake has some of the strongest venom on Earth. It uses it to feed on other deadly snakes, including cobras.

PRETTY IN POO

Rainbow scarab beetles are hard to miss. Their bright green, red, purple and gold bodies **shimmer**. These shiny insects hang out somewhere disgusting – on poo! Female scarab beetles lay their eggs in animal poo. Newly hatched **larvae** eat it. The beetle's nasty meal choice helps to clean the ground.

CREEPING CRABS

Halloween crabs are dressed up and ready to trick-or-treat. They are spooky colours like red, purple and black. And they only come out at night. The crabs creep along the forest floor. Then they drag leaves back to their homes.

EIGHT-LEGGED DANCERS

Peacock spiders are tiny. They are smaller than the rubber on a pencil. But males show off colourful designs on their fanlike tails. These jumping spiders dance to attract females. Check out those fancy tail colours as they move and groove.

FACT
Peacock spiders only live in Australia.

GLOSSARY

cell one of the tiny building blocks that make up the bodies of all plants and animals

coral reef an underwater structure made up of the hardened bodies of corals; corals are small, colourful sea creatures

larva an insect at the stage of development between an egg and an adult

neon extremely bright

shimmer to shine or sparkle

spine a long, pointed growth

venom a poisonous liquid produced by some animals

READ MORE

BOOKS

Animal Adaptations (Engage Literacy), Ruth Bjorkland (Raintree, 2017)

Animal Adaptations (Engineered by Nature), Louise Spilsbury (Raintree, 2020)

Colourful Kingdom, Anna Omedes (Orange Mosquito, 2022)

WEBSITES

Animal Camouflage
kids.kiddle.co/Camouflage

Protective Colouration
kids.britannica.com/kids/article/protective-coloration/353670

INDEX

ABOUT THE AUTHOR

Megan Cooley Peterson has been an avid reader and writer since she was a little girl. She has written non-fiction children's books about topics ranging from urban legends to gross animal facts. She lives in Minnesota, USA, with her husband and daughter.